MY
BOOK
OF
ANIMALS

WEEKLY READER BOOKS,
MIDDLETOWN, CONNECTICUT.

MY BOOK OF ANIMALS

MY BOOK OF ANIMALS

Editors
Rita Gould
Elizabeth Steinkamp
Ingrid Goldsmid
Rachael Jones

This special edition prepared for
Weekly Reader Books
by Autumn Publishing Limited
Chichester, West Sussex, England.

Copyright © Presse Bureau Junior
ISBN 0 94659 310 8
Typeset by Words&Spaces, Rowlands Castle, Hants, UK
Printed in Belgium

CONTENTS

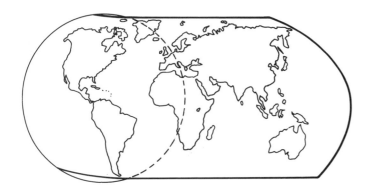

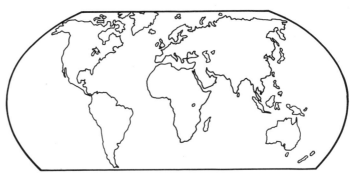

EUROPE

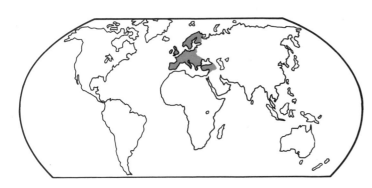

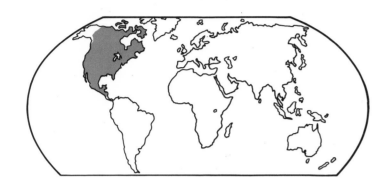

NORTH AMERICA

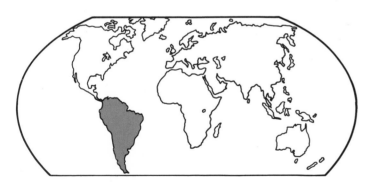

SOUTH AMERICA

ASIA

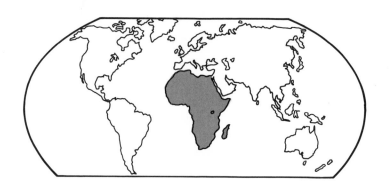

AFRICA

OCEANIA

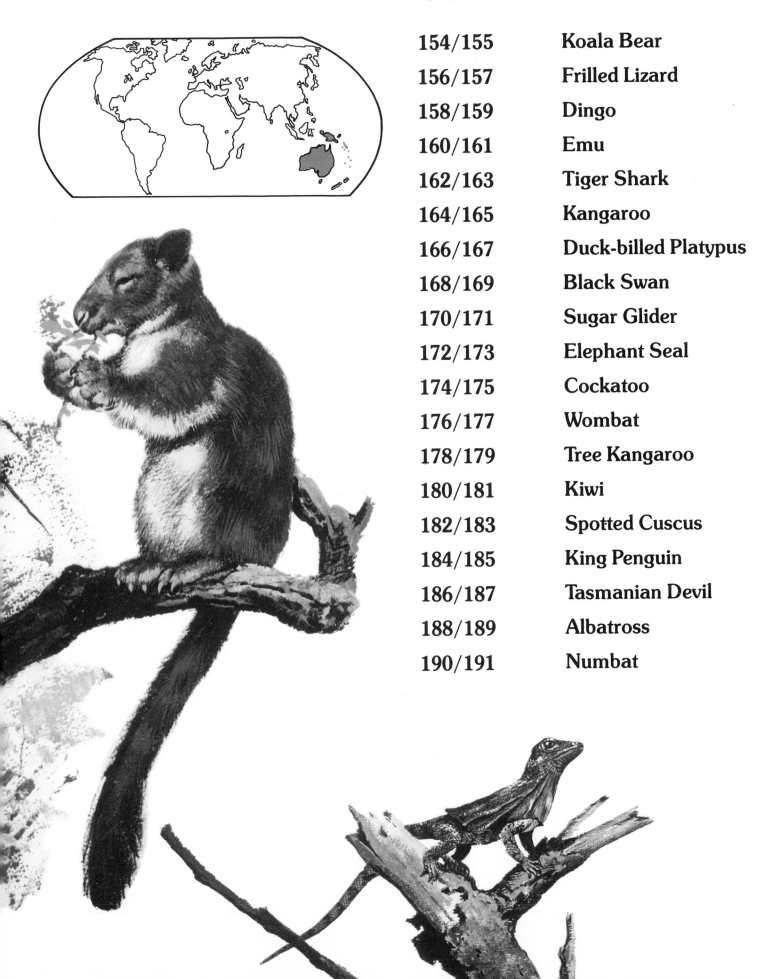

Introduction

There are thousands of different creatures in our world. There are creatures that fly, swim, climb and dig. Each one is part of a family that has lived on the earth for thousands and thousands of years. During that time, the animals have changed and developed until each one is perfectly suited to the environment in which it lives. The polar bear in the cold lands of the Artic and the camel living in the deserts of Africa are examples of how creatures can survive in the harshest of places.

In *My Book of Animals* you will find out about just a few of the amazing creatures on our planet. You will learn where these animals live and what they eat. Illustrations will show you how the grown animals and their babies look.

It is a sad thing that some of these creatures are in danger of becoming

extinct. Animals are extinct when there are none of that particular creature left in the world. Tragically, once an animal has become extinct, it can never be replaced.

What are these animals in danger from? Their main enemy is people. Humans need more and more of the world to grow crops to feed themselves and to build houses to shelter their families. However, new farms or towns mean that there is less room for the animals that used to live there. Polluted air and water, by-products of human settlements, also affect the well-being of animals.

Happily, nowadays people have come to realize that they must share the earth with animals. A lot of work is being done to save the rare animals and it is hoped that creatures like the giant panda, the bald eagle, and the whale will be able to live in peace and safety.

Europe

The puffin

The puffin is easy to recognize because of its colorful beak. In winter the beak is red and brown, but then changes to a bright yellow with streaks of red and blue.

Puffins live together in large groups called colonies. They are very good swimmers. They can dive as deep as thirty feet and stay underwater for one to two minutes.

The male puffin scoops out a nest under a rock. The female lays one egg and sits on it for nearly six weeks. Puffin parents take great care of their chick when it hatches. They bring lots of fish to help their offspring grow strong.

When the chick is old enough, the parents will leave it. On its own, the young puffin finds its way to the sea to catch fish.

Europe

The wildcat

The wildcat looks like a tame, tabby cat, but even the smallest wildcat kitten will snarl and spit at a stranger.

Wildcat kittens are born in April, and for a few weeks they stay in their den. As soon as they are strong enough, their mother teaches them how to hunt for their own food. Wildcats live in lonely parts of the mountains. They are not seen very often as they hunt at night.

They will hunt small animals, birds and fish, and also sick or injured animals. Farmers do not like them because they sometimes attack the sheep in the pens.

The wildcat has a broad head and is striped like a domestic tabby cat. However, it is very fierce and will attack without hesitation.

15

Europe

The red deer

The red deer is a shy animal that comes out in the evenings to feed on young leaves. Deer eat crops such as wheat and oats, carrots and beets, and so they are not very popular with farmers.

Red deer babies, or calves, are able to run soon after they are born. If the female, or doe, smells danger, she signals to the calf and it immediately crouches down and stays very still. Male red deer, or stags, start to grow antlers on their heads during their first winter. The antlers of a full-grown stag can be over three feet long and weigh over twenty pounds.

Red deer calves are dappled with white spots on reddish-brown fur. This coloring helps them hide in the bushes.

17

Europe

The otter

The otter lives on the bank of a river or lake and spends most of its time in the water. It is a very good swimmer and catches most of its food in the water.

An otter's fur is short and thick. As the otter grows older, its fur becomes oily. This helps to keep the fur waterproof, which is very important for a water animal. An otter also has a layer of fat under its skin. This helps to keep it warm in cold weather.

An otter's home is called a holt. The entrance is underwater, so it is very hard to find. There is a room above the water level where, in May, two to five cubs are born.

An otter uses its webbed hind feet as oars and its tail to steer as it twists and turns in the water.

Europe

The white stork

The white stork spends the winter in warm southern countries. In the summer it flies back to the same site where it nested the year before. The male stork brings twigs, rags, paper and dirt to the female, who repairs and feathers the nest until it is like new.

Storks feed on small fish or on animals that live on damp ground or in marshes. They stand very still and suddenly stretch their long necks to catch their prey in their pointed beaks.

Storks are thought to be lucky, and some people are very pleased if a pair of storks makes a nest on the roof of their house.

A stork often stands on one leg, drawing the other up into its feathers to keep warm. Stork chicks grow very quickly. The parents have to make the walls of the nest higher so the babies do not fall out.

Europe

The pine marten

The pine marten is a small, fierce weasel that lives in pine forests. It is very good at climbing trees, and can move so quietly that its prey does not hear it coming. A pine marten eats all sorts of small animals, and also enjoys fruits such as wild cherries and blackberries.

A pair of pine martens find a dry hole and line it with dried grass and leaves. Pine marten babies are born in April. They stay in their dens until June or July, when they are strong enough to look after themselves.

If a pine marten meets an animal which is larger or fiercer than itself, it will cling to a branch and pretend to be dead.

Europe

The Alpine ibex

The Alpine ibex lives in the cold, rocky mountains of Europe.

This sure-footed animal can move easily and confidently, leaping from rock to rock among the cliffs and crags. It feeds on the tough and spiky tussock grass that grows high in the mountains.

The females and young live together in herds on the lower slopes where the food is more plentiful. The older males spend most of their time higher up. They can balance on the narrowest ledge and remain completely still for hours.

Like its descendant, the domestic goat, the ibex has short legs and powerful horns. In the winter its coat grows darker and thicker to keep it warm.

Within a few hours of its birth in May or June, the baby ibex can move confidently over the rocks. By the time the winter comes, it is ready to face the snow and gales that sweep over the mountains.

Europe

The hedgehog

The hedgehog has a coat of brown hair and spines. If it is disturbed, it will raise its spines to make a sharp wall, or even curl itself into a ball. Dogs or foxes do not often attack hedgehogs, because they soon learn that they will get a pricked nose!

Hedgehogs are nocturnal, which means that they sleep during the day and come out at night to hunt. They eat slugs and snails, insects, worms, frogs, mice and birds' eggs. Hedgehogs can even eat poisonous snakes, because the poison does not harm them.

Hedgehogs hibernate, or sleep during the winter in a nest made of moss and leaves which they build in a sheltered spot under a hedge.

Baby hedgehogs are blind when they are born. Their spines are soft and they cannot curl up into balls like their parents.

27

Europe

The loggerhead turtle

The loggerhead turtle is a reptile. Tortoises, terrapins and turtles are also reptiles. Like birds, reptiles lay eggs, but they are not warm blooded creatures like birds and mammals. The loggerhead turtle is about three feet long and lives in warm seas. There, it hunts for the fish and shell-fish which make up its diet.

Although she spends her life in the sea, the female turtle lays her eggs on land. She drags herself up the beach, digs a hole in the sand and lays up to a hundred eggs. Then she covers the eggs and swims back out to sea.

28

Loggerhead turtles have no claws on their flippers as some turtles do. Their limbs are adapted for swimming, and they cannot walk very well on land.

Squirrels sit up on their hind legs, balancing on their bushy tails, and holding food in their front paws. They like to eat acorns, pine seeds, beech nuts and leaf buds.

Europe

The squirrel

Squirrels are found all over the world and usually live in wooded areas. Their strong legs, and long, flexible fingers and claws help them to scamper up and down the trees and leap from branch to branch. They use their long, bushy tails to balance themselves as they jump, and to wrap around for warmth.

During September and October, squirrels start to collect nuts to hide away for the winter. Squirrels hibernate during the very cold months, which means that they sleep most of the time. When they wake up, they search for the nuts hidden earlier in the year.

The female squirrel builds a nest, or drey, in the fork of a tree between two branches. The nest is made of twigs and leaves. A round top on the nest keeps out rain.

Europe

The dolphin

The common dolphin is a member of the whale family, and is found in all seas, except those which are very cold. It will swim with many others in a group of up to a thousand. The group, or school, hunts shoals of herring and sardines.

Dolphins are very playful. Sometimes a school of dolphins will suddenly leap clear of the water and fall back with a great splash.

Dolphins are very intelligent. They can solve simple problems, and can possibly even use a kind of language to 'speak' to one another.

Because dolphins are mammals, they do not lay eggs. The babies are born in the sea and drink milk from their mothers.

Dolphins often follow in the wake of a ship. Long ago, sailors believed that dolphins would carry them to shore if they fell overboard.

A badger's set has several tunnels and living areas lined with dried grass or straw. Badgers are tidy creatures and keep their homes very clean.

Europe

The badger

The badger can be recognized by the two black lines running from its nose over its ears and merging into its coat.

Badgers are nocturnal animals. They sleep in their dens during the day and come out to feed at night. Badgers eat fruit, insects, voles, moles and worms. They are also very fond of honey.

The badger lives in a burrow, or set, under the ground. The badger is very good at digging, and uses its powerful fore paws, strong claws and strong back legs to clear away the soil.

Badgers do not hibernate during the winter, and will stay in their sets only during the coldest weather.

Europe

The brown bear

The brown bear lives in forests. It is very good at climbing trees to rob the wild bees' nests of the honey which it loves. The brown bear also likes to eat fruit and crops, and is expert at scooping fish out of the water with its paws.

Brown bears eat very well during the summer to build up a layer of fat under their skins. They hibernate in dry caves in winter, and the fat keeps them warm and alive.

The largest brown bear is the grizzly bear of North America. It can grow to be over nine feet long and weigh over five hundred pounds.

One or two cubs are born during the winter. They are taken care of by the mother bear, since the father does not stay with his mate and babies.

Europe

The red fox

With its red-brown coat and long, bushy tail, or brush, the fox is easily recognizable. During the day, the fox stays out of sight in its den or earth. The dens have more than one exit, so that the fox can escape in times of danger.

In the late evening, the fox comes out to hunt. It has very sharp eyesight and hearing and a good sense of smell. This helps it to catch the birds, moles, rabbits, field mice and voles that it eats. Farmers say that a fox will creep into the hen houses and steal chickens.

Foxes are very adaptable creatures. Many are found living in towns, where they feed on scraps of food left in garbage pails.

Fox cubs are born in early spring. The female, or vixen, looks after them until they are six months old, and teaches them how to survive.

Europe

The falcon

The falcon is a very fast and efficient bird of prey. They have hooked beaks, curved talons for catching their prey, and very keen eyesight.

Falcons can be trained to catch birds in flight and then return to their owner. There are several kinds of falcons, one of which is called the peregrine. The peregrine is one of the fastest-flying falcons, and can reach great heights. The word 'peregrine' means 'traveling' – and the peregrine does travel. It migrates for thousands of miles over Europe and Africa each winter.

In the spring, the falcon flies back to its nesting site among rocks, or at the top of a tall tree. The hen, or female, falcon sits on her eggs while the male hunts for food. When the chicks are born, both parents are kept busy bringing them food.

Peregrine chicks are large and fluffy, with sharp, hooked beaks. The parents chew the meat to soften it before giving it to their chicks.

Europe

The mallard duck

The mallard is at home on almost every town or city pond, but it can also be found on estuaries and along the shoreline. It will gather with hundreds, or even thousands, of other ducks in large flocks.

Mallards usually feed on plants, insects and small water creatures which live near the surface of the water. Sometimes they will dive under the water to search for food.

The duck's feathers are kept waterproof by a special oil that is produced by a gland on the tail. Using its beak, the duck covers all its feathers with the oil. This is called preening.

The male, or drake, is very colorful. He has a glossy green head with a white band around his neck, a brown breast and a violet-blue patch on each wing. His beak is yellow and his webbed feet are orange-red. The drake loses his colorful feathers in June and cannot fly for two months until they grow back.

The female is not as colorful as the male. because she has to hide in the reeds on her nest. She lines the nest with soft feathers. called down. that she plucks from her own breast.

Europe

The brown hare

The brown hare has strong back legs, which help it to run very fast and to leap up to twenty feet in one bound. A hare has been recorded as running at over forty miles per hour. This speed is very important, because the hare has many enemies, such as the weasel and the fox. The hare is always on the alert for danger, and its long ears twitch in all directions, constantly listening for its enemies. Its eyes are large, and set on the sides of the head. The hare does not need to move its eyes or head to look around, because it can see forward, backward, upward and sideway at the same time.

Hares mainly eat at night. They feed on grass, clover and many kinds of fruit and vegetables.

The hare's den, or form, is usually no more than a slight hollow in the ground protected by long grass. Baby hares are called leverets.

44

Europe

The stoat

The stoat is a very good hunter. Its paws have fur underneath, so that it can move without making any noise. The stoat is so slim that it can slip into narrow cracks between rocks to catch its prey. Long whiskers help it to feel where it is going, and it has a very keen sense of smell.

In summer, the stoat's coat is a rusty brown color. In winter, the coat turns pure white, except for the tip of the tail. This helps the stoat to hide in the snow.

Baby stoats are born in a den deep under a rock. At first they are helpless, but soon they are able to follow their mother and learn to hunt for themselves.

If danger threatens, the mother stoat will carry her babies one by one to safety.

North America

The American bison

The American bison is usually called a buffalo. It is a large, heavy animal, which may weigh over a ton and stand over six feet high at the shoulder. Bison also live in South Africa, Europe and in the East. The American buffalo is usually heavier than other bison.

Nowadays the bison's main enemy is the wolf, but a hundred years ago men hunted it until there were very few of these creatures left. The huge herds, hunted for sport and food, were nearly destroyed. Now their numbers are growing again, since laws have been passed to protect the bison from hunters.

The bison's heavy coat protects it during the cold winter months, when blizzards and snow storms rage over the plains.

North America

The beaver

The beaver is a water animal that is a natural engineer. It creates its own ponds by cutting down trees to dam streams. It also digs canals to float logs to its dams. With its strong front teeth, a beaver gnaws into a tree trunk until it crashes to the ground. In the center of the pond, behind the dam, the beaver builds a home or lodge of branches and twigs. It is cemented together with mud and grass.

The beaver slaps this into place with its paddle-like tail. Beavers also use their homes to store food for their families.

At one time, beavers were found all across Europe, as well as in North America and Canada. However, they have been hunted for their fur and now they are rare in Europe. In places where there are very few beavers, they do not build dams but live in holes in river banks.

When the beaver gnaws at the trees in the water, special membranes close so that no water gets into its ears and nose.

The eagle's nest, or aerie, is built in a tall tree or on a high cliff. Baby eagles are called eaglets. They are about four months old before they leave the nest to hunt for themselves.

North America

The bald eagle

The bald eagle is a symbol of courage and is the national emblem of the United States. Sadly, it nearly disappeared from its usual range. Why? Because people destroyed many of its nesting sites and polluted the rivers, leaving few fish for it to feed on.

The eagle family contains some of the most powerful of all the living birds. The bald eagle has a wing span of seven to eight feet. It can soar high into the sky and glide on the wind currents without beating its wings.

The bald eagle is not really bald, but its head is white, as is its tail. The other feathers are brown, and the wings are edged with white.

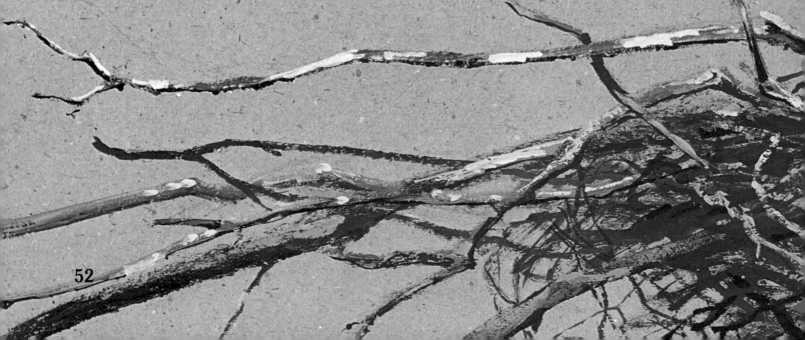

North America

The snowshoe rabbit

Snowshoe rabbits live in burrows in woods, open valleys or on the lower slopes of hills. They stay in their burrows during the day, coming out in early morning and late evening to feed. They eat all the grass around the burrows, cropping it short with their long, sharp front teeth.

All rabbits have many enemies. The snowshoe rabbit escapes from its hunters because it has large hind legs, which help it to run over the snow drifts without sinking.

Extra hair, which grows on its feet, helps the rabbit to grip the slippery snow and ice more easily.

In the winter, the snowshoe rabbit's fur turns white, and it can hide against the snow.

Snowshoe rabbits have two litters of babies a year. Three or four young are born in the spring and the same number again in the fall.

North America

The walrus

The walrus lives in the icy waters of North America and the Arctic Circle. It likes to swim where the bottom of the sea is mostly made up of gravel. It uses its long tusks to stir the gravel up, and then sorts out the food using its sensitive whiskers and lips.

Walruses are usually peaceful creatures, but they do not hesitate to use their sharp tusks as weapons if they are attacked.

Male walruses are called bulls, and females are called cows. However, their babies are not called calves but pups. It is thought that their ancestors must have been very closely related to early dogs.

Under its skin, the walrus grows a thick layer of fat, called blubber, which helps keep it warm in the cold seas.

An adult bull walrus can grow to a length of fifteen feet and weigh over three thousand pounds.

Baby raccoons are born in the spring.
They live in their den for about a year,
during which time they learn how to
take care of themselves.

North America

The raccoon

Raccoons are easily recognizable by the black 'masks' over their eyes, and their striped tails. They eat insects, frogs, mice, wild fruit and berries. Raccoons always live near rivers and streams, because they have to soak their food in water before they can eat it. Their tiny fore paws have flexible fingers which the raccoons use to catch their food.

Raccoons are able to adapt to a changing environment. They are as much at home in towns, stealing scraps from garbage cans, as in quiet woodlands.

North America

The coyote

With its bushy tail and long, pointed ears, the coyote looks very similar to a fox, but in fact it is a small wolf. It lives on the plains of North America, where it hunts ground squirrels and rodents. Farmers say it steals chickens and kills new born lambs, so the coyote is often hunted. However, experts say that the coyote does more good by eating rodents than it does harm by killing the farmers' animals.

In the evening, coyotes let out their hunting call. This is a long, sad howl followed by a series of short yelps. Other coyotes answer until the plain is alive with their hunting cries

A coyote cub will become tame very quickly if it is captured when young. It accepts most food and likes to make friends with other domestic animals.

North America

The fur seal

The fur seal is an expert swimmer and can turn and twist in the water while chasing fish. It can even swim backward, which no fish can do. On land, the fur seal is more clumsy. Some seals cannot use their back flippers on land, but the fur seal's hind flippers turn forward and help it walk. It can even gallop a short distance if it needs to.

The male, or bull, fur seal weighs between 350 and 600 pounds, and grows six feet long. The females are about five feet long.

In the spring, thousands of fur seals come on shore as this is the time when the pups are born. For five to six months, the islands around Alaska are covered with fur seals until it is time for them to go back to sea once more.

Baby fur seals enjoy playing with other pups, often using their parents as slides and hiding places.

North America

The caribou

The reindeer of Northern Europe and the caribou of North America are very closely related. They are the only members of the deer family where the females also grow horns.

The caribou is well suited for the cold climate in which it lives, because it has a thick coat and a hairy nose. Its hooves are broad and deeply cleft so that they spread on snow and give the caribou more support.

In winter caribou scrape the snow away from the frozen ground to find reindeer moss to eat. In summer, they feed on leaves, grass and water plants. The herds of caribou make long journeys of several hundred miles from their winter to their summer feeding grounds and always follow the same route.

The caribou's main enemy is the wolf. If attacked, the caribou will use its long, widespread antlers to defend itself.

North America

The polar bear

The white-furred polar bear is the best known of the animals that live in the Arctic region. It is one of the largest and fiercest bears and feeds on seals that it catches sleeping on the edge of the ice.

Polar bears are very good swimmers and expert divers. They have been seen swimming strongly 200 miles out from land.

In the worst of the winter, polar bears find a sheltered hole or ice cave and sleep, waking up from time to time to feed.

Polar bear cubs stay with their mother for about three years. During this time they are taught everything they need to know to survive in the very cold Arctic climate.

North America

The skunk

Skunks are found only in the woodlands of the Americas.

They are famous for their only means of defense. If a skunk is attacked, it will turn its back, lift its tail into the air and squirt a foul smelling jet of liquid into its enemy's face. The smell lasts for days, and the liquid is so powerful that it can cause blindness if it goes directly into the eyes.

The skunk is also very recognizable because of its black and white coloring and its bushy tail.

Skunks stay in their burrows during the day and come out at dusk to search for worms, insects, birds, birds' eggs, and small rodents such as mice and rats.

Skunks walk about with their tails in the air, warning their enemies of their foul smelling weapon.

North America

The prairie dog

The prairie dog is really a type of squirrel. It does not live in trees but, with thousands of its companions, digs huge burrows, or cities, under the prairies of North America. One city covered 24,000 square miles and 400 million prairie dogs lived there.

Every now and then, a band of prairie dogs sets off across the plains to dig a new city. This prevents the old burrow from becoming overcrowded.

Prairie dogs have many enemies, and they have look-outs on constant alert for danger. If these guards see a coyote or an eagle, they alert the others with a barking sound. This alarm sends all the prairie dogs running for cover. This barking noise is why they were called prairie dogs by the first settlers.

The prairie dog eats grass, and also chews off any tall plants that might give cover to an enemy.

North America

The sperm whale

The whale is the largest animal alive today. There are two kinds of whale: the whalebone whales and the toothed whale. The largest of the toothed whales is the sperm whale, which can grow to be about sixty feet long. It has a mouth full of sharp teeth, some as long as eight inches. Sperm whales feed mainly on squid.

The whale is a sea creature and looks like a fish, but it is a mammal. This means that it is warm-blooded, gives birth to live babies and feeds them on milk. A baby sperm whale is nearly twelve feet long and is as large as an elephant.

Scientists believe that whales can 'talk' to each other by making a series of echoing noises which travel long distances under the water.

74

South America

The blue and yellow macaw

Macaws live in the tropical forests and jungles of South America. They are members of the parrot family and are very brightly colored with blue and yellow feathers. They have been hunted so much in the past that they are now quite rare.

Macaws like to eat Brazil nuts, which have very hard shells. However, macaws have extremely sharp beaks and can easily break the nuts. Macaws are timid birds. If they see a stranger coming through the forest, they will perch on a branch and shriek as loudly as possible to warn other animals of danger.

Some macaws are the same size as a pigeon. Other types can grow to be over three feet long.

75

Sloths do not have to find water to drink, as they get all the liquid they need from the leaves they eat.

South America

The two-toed sloth

The sloth lives in South America. There are several different types, but they all move very slowly, and usually prefer to live in trees, rarely coming down to the ground.

The two-toed sloth has two sharp, hooked claws on its fore paws. It uses these to walk upside down, clinging to the tree branches. Sloths are also able to sleep upside down.

The claws on their feet make it difficult for sloths to move on the ground, so they look very uncomfortable if they have to travel along the forest floor. However, they have no fear of water, and are good swimmers.

South America

The Patagonian cavy

The Patagonian cavy is a rodent that lives on the plains of South America. It is related to the guinea pig and also to the hare. It has long back legs like a hare, a broad face and soft, strong fur. Cavies are just over one foot long when they are fully grown.

Cavies are very timid creatures. If one is frightened, it will rush off without looking where it is going. Cavies can be so blind with panic that they will bump into anything in their way.

Cavy babies are able to run very soon after they are born. There are usually two litters a year, and one or two babies are born each time.

South America

The guanaco

The guanaco lives on the plains and in the mountains of South America. It is a member of the camel family, as its long neck and head show. Its body is covered with a thick coat of reddish brown and white hair. Its fur is much prized by the South Americans, who use it to make their clothing. The guanaco is also hunted for its meat.

It is said that when a guanaco becomes ill, it wanders off by itself to a lonely spot to die.

There are several other members of the camel family in South America. The llama has been domesticated for hundreds of years. Alpaca are raised because they provide very fine wool.

South America

The jaguar

The jaguar lives in the forests of South America and is the largest member of the American cat family. Ringed spots in a pattern on its sides and back make the jaguar look a bit like a panther.

The jaguar will cover many miles a day in search of its prey. Even a mother with her cubs will cover several miles. It will eat almost any meat, and will not hesitate to attack humans if it is hungry or trapped.

Jaguars are very good climbers. The cubs are taught at a young age how to reach the top branches of a tree to steal from birds' nests.

South Americans call the jaguar a 'tiger'. It is smaller than a tiger, but is just as fierce.

Asia

The Arctic fox

The Arctic fox lives by the ice-covered ocean in the northern part of the world. The temperature there does not rise much above freezing, even in the summer.

During the short summer, the Arctic fox's coat is brown. The brown coat helps to camouflage the fox against the ground. During the winter, the fox grows a very thick coat of white fur, which protects it against the cold and also enables it to hide against the snow drifts.

Arctic foxes hunt for food even during the coldest weather. The foxes hunt alone, following polar bears to steal scraps from their kills. They also catch small creatures called lemmings and store them in the cracks in rocks to eat during the long winter.

Baby foxes are born in May in a den scraped out of the snow.
They stay with their mother until the following winter.

Asia

The wild ass

The wild ass is related to the donkey. It is a strong, intelligent animal which will attack any enemy that threatens the foals.

Wild asses live in herds and each member of the herd has its own job. Two or three males stay with the she-asses and foals, guarding them from danger. Other males go on ahead to search for fresh pastures.

The asses have very good eyesight, and sensitive hooves that can feel the vibrations of wolves approaching from far away. This gives them time to escape to high, rocky ledges where the wolves cannot follow. This animal can run quickly and can reach speeds of forty miles an hour.

86

The she-ass gives birth in a quiet place, but as soon as the baby can move around they rejoin the herd.

Asia

The argali

The argali is a wild sheep that lives in the mountains of central Asia. The male grows a pair of large curving horns. During the mating season, the males charge at each other, and their horns meet with a jarring crash. Sometimes the battles go on for days, but neither animal seems to win or lose.

The males, or rams, use their horns to frighten away other animals from their territory. If they see an enemy, the rams let out frightening bellows, and the females or ewes stamp out a warning before leading their lambs to safety.

Argali use a series of whistles and bleats to 'talk' to one another. Lambs learn these sounds before they are allowed to explore unfamiliar places on their own.

The argali is said to be the ancestor of the domestic sheep.

Asia

The peacock

The peacock is the male peafowl, which is a very large type of pheasant. His feathers are some of the most colorful in the bird world – blue, green, purple and orange. The tail feathers are long and flowing, and the peacock spreads them to show a magnificent fan, decorated with what look like eyes.

The female peafowl is called the peahen.

She does not have the brilliant coloring or magnificent tail of the male. She takes care of the chicks, and so she has to blend into the undergrowth.

There are two types of peafowl. The blue peacock comes from India and Sri Lanka, and the green peacock lives in Burma, China and Malaysia. The blue species has been tamed for two thousand years.

The chicks are so well developed when they hatch that within a few days they can fly up into the trees to roost with their mother.

Asia

The macaque

The macaque is a monkey that lives on the islands in the north of Japan. The climate is very cold on these islands, and the macaque has developed a thick coat to protect it from the freezing weather.

Macaques are very intelligent and are able to learn from each other. A few years ago, scientists noticed that one female macaque was washing her food in the river. Some years later, the whole tribe was doing it. In this land of snow and ice, hot pools are found, and the monkeys often spend hours in the warm water.

At night the males guard the mothers and babies, who huddle together for protection against their enemies.

Asia

The giant panda

Giant pandas live in the bamboo forests in southwest China and Tibet. They are a rare species, because their natural habitat is becoming smaller and smaller as man cuts down the forests. Some have been captured in the hope that they will breed, but pandas do not breed well in captivity. One reason may be that pandas need a lot of space.

The giant panda eats fish and small animals, but its favorite food is bamboo shoots. Bamboo has sharp edges, so a protective horny skin grows over the panda's windpipe.

Pandas do not hibernate in winter, but find shelter in trees.

The giant panda looks like a cuddly black and white bear, but in fact it is related to the raccoon.

Asia

The snow leopard

The snow leopard is the rarest member of the family of big cats. It lives in the treeless, mountainous areas of central Asia.

Snow leopards have thick, soft fur with a yellow sheen and dark markings on a gray background. These leopards are very rare because they are widely hunted for their beautiful fur.

Snow leopards feed on meat, and their main prey are the wild sheep and goats that also live in the mountains. Each snow leopard family has its own territory. No strange leopard is allowed to enter. The leopards will fight any intruder who dares to come in.

Another name for the snow leopard is the ounce.

Asia

The orangutan

The orangutan is a member of the ape family. It is large and powerful, yet quiet. It looks very human. In fact, the name 'orangutan' means 'man of the woods'. Orangutans have gray-brown skin and rusty red hair, short legs and very long arms that reach nearly to their ankles.

The orangutan lives in the forests of southeast Asia. It uses its long arms to swing through the trees in which it lives. It feeds on young leaves, blossoms and fruit. Although it is such a large animal, an orangutan will spend most of its life in the trees. A male adult can weigh as much as 220 pounds, so it always tests branches before putting its weight on them.

The orangutan sleeps in the trees. It builds a nest in the fork of a tree to rest and may use it for only one night.

99

Asia

The tiger

Tigers prefer to live by themselves. They hunt all kinds of animals, from insects and fish to deer and even baby elephants.

A tigress, or female tiger, will find a cave hidden behind some rocks where her cubs will be born. She has to find a safe spot because tiger cubs are completely helpless when they are newborn. They are not able to see until they are two weeks old. By the time they are six months old, the cubs are ready to learn to hunt for themselves. They finally leave their mother when they are two years old.

The biggest tigers in the world are found in the cold lands of Siberia, and have long gray coats instead of the striped fur of their smaller Asian cousins. The tigers that live in tropical countries hate the heat, and will stay in a stream or river for most of the day to keep cool. Unlike other members of the cat family, they have no fear of water and are good swimmers. Another difference is that they are not very good at climbing.

Tigers dislike the heat, and will stay in a stream or river for most of the day to keep cool.

The Indian rhinoceros

The rhinoceros's horn is not made of bone, but of matted hair. The baby rhinoceros has a shiny patch on its snout to show where the hair will start to develop. It takes several years for the horn to grow fully.

A rhinoceros's skin is very thick, and deep folds cover its neck and legs. Ticks and insects lay their eggs in the folds. The rhinoceros bathes often, sinking down into the water to wash the eggs away. The tick bird is the rhinoceros's friend. It hops up and down the rhinoceros's back, picking the insects off with its beak.

The rhinoceros looks clumsy but it can gallop at a surprising speed and turn with agility — especially when charging an enemy.

Asia

The Bactrian camel

The Bactrian camel lives in deserts where the heat can be unbearable. The camel can live in these places because it does not lose moisture by sweating.

In the summer, herds of camels go up into the hills to look for better grazing. They may climb as high as 9000 feet in search of food. In winter they return to the desert. Salt is very important to camels, because they use it to keep moisture in their bodies. They find the salt in dried up water holes and lakes.

The Bactrian camel has two humps on its back. Its cousin, the Arabian camel or dromedary, has one hump and does not grow such a thick coat.

The lesser panda

The lesser panda lives in the Himalayan mountains and is related to the giant panda. Unlike the giant panda, the lesser panda has a long, bushy tail which is striped like a raccoon's. As its name suggests, the lesser panda is smaller than its Chinese cousin. It grows to about three feet including the tail, which is fifteen to eighteen inches long.

The lesser panda has a thick, soft, glossy coat. The rusty brown coat has a touch of yellow and is black underneath. The higher the animal lives in the mountains, the thicker the fur grows.

Lesser pandas eat mostly leaves and berries, but they also search for insects and birds' eggs.

The lesser panda uses its sharp claws to hang on to tree branches.

Asia

The blackbuck

The blackbuck is a member of the antelope family. The male is a very handsome animal. It has a shiny, dark coat with white underneath and a pair of very long, twisted horns. The female, or doe, has a plain, yellow-brown coat and no horns at all.

Blackbucks live on the open plains. There is always a blackbuck on guard.

It keeps a sharp lookout and uses its keen sense of hearing to protect the herd from enemies. If a tiger tries to creep up, the sentry leaps high into the air as a warning. The herd runs away so fast that few animals can catch up. The blackbuck is one of the fastest land animals in the world.

When the herd moves to find new pastures, the fawns lead the way. Other blackbucks of the same age bunch together in their own groups.

Asia

The rhinoceros hornbill

The rhinoceros hornbill gets its name from the horny lump on top of its thick bill. The horn is bright yellow and red, and so strong that it can be carved like ivory.

When it is nearly time for the female to lay her eggs, she looks for a hole in a hollow tree and cleans it out. After she has settled in, the male collects lumps of mud and fills up the entrance except for a small hole. The mother hatches her chicks and stays with them for three months while the father feeds the whole family. When it is time for the young to leave the nest, the mother and father chip away at the hard dried mud until it cracks.

The hornbill lives in flocks of five or six. It does not fly very often, and when it does, it looks very heavy and clumsy.

Asia

The Indian elephant

The Indian elephant grows to a height of about ten feet and weighs up to four tons. This elephant is easy to tame and to train and works in the forests moving logs and stones.

When a baby elephant is born, a female elephant helps the mother until she and her newborn calf are ready to rejoin the herd. The herd is guarded by the bull elephants, who are ready to protect their young against any enemy.

Elephants are very fond of water. They will lie down and wallow in the river and squirt trunkfuls of cool water over themselves.

When it is born, the baby elephant has a rough, hairy coat and looks likes its ancestor, the mammoth.

Asia

The tapir

Tapirs look as though they are some sort of pig. In fact, they are closely related to the rhinoceros.

Like the rhinoceros, the tapir loves the water and can swim very well. It can spend several minutes under the water before coming up for air. If a tapir is disturbed by a leopard or tiger, it will fight fiercely and then escape into the water nearby.

A baby tapir's coat is spotted and striped, but these markings disappear before the baby is a year old. The black and white coloring of the adult tapir makes it very difficult to see in the shadowy jungle.

At night, tapirs graze on plants growing by the water's edge.

Asia

The gayal

The gayal lives in the hills of northwest India. It can be tamed, and is then raised for its meat, milk and wool. Although gayals can be tamed, they could turn wild again at any time and disappear back into the forests.

Gayals stay in the shade of the bushes during the day, coming out to drink when it is cooler. It is at this time that they are most open to attack from tigers and other meat eaters. However, the bulls or male gayals are always on the alert. With their heads down, they charge at the enemy.

When the calves are old enough, the herd of gayals migrate to find fresh feeding grounds.

Asia

The loris

The loris is related to the monkey family and lives in the forests of Malaysia. It sleeps all through the day, rolled into a ball on a branch. At night, it comes out to feed on fruit or any insect, bird or reptile that it can creep up on.

The loris looks very fragile with its skinny arms and legs, and large staring eyes. But it is really very strong. A loris can grip a branch so tightly that it will not fall off even when it sleeps.

The female loris carries her babies wherever she goes. They cling to her fur and do not let go for several months.

The word 'loris' is Dutch, and it means 'clown'. It certainly suits this funny-looking animal.

Africa

The crocodile

The crocodile is a reptile, descended from the dinosaurs of long ago. It is a cold-blooded creature, which spends much of its time basking in the sun on the shores of the lakes and rivers of Africa. The female crocodile scoops a hole in the sand and lays up to one hundred eggs. She then covers the eggs with sand, but she visits them regularly to make sure that they are still safe. The sand heats up under the sun, and so the eggs are kept warm until it is time for the babies to hatch.

The crocodile has a strange friend, a bird called the blacksmith plover. This little bird pecks scraps of food and insects out of the crocodile's mouth. Why? It cleans the reptile's teeth and feeds itself at the same time.

120

Crocodiles keep on growing all their lives. Some measure up to twenty feet in length.

121

Africa

The cheetah

The cheetah is the fastest animal on land. From a standstill, it can reach a speed of over forty miles an hour in less than two seconds. It can run up to seventy miles an hour for short distances.

Cheetahs have long bodies and slender legs. Its claws do not retract, that is, do not go back into the paws like other members of the cat family.

When a cheetah is hunting, it selects its prey, for example, an antelope, and stalks it for a long time before the final rush. It does not make a kill every time. Sometimes the antelope is able to outrun the cheetah, which cannot keep up its speed for very long.

The cheetah grows to a length of four to five feet, and its tail is about two-and-a-half to three feet long.

During the Middle Ages, eastern princes tamed cheetahs to hunt for them.

 124

Africa

The giraffe

The giraffe is the tallest animal in the world, growing to a height of eighteen feet. It uses its long neck to reach and eat the top leaves of the acacia tree, its main food.

When the giraffe wants a drink, it has to slowly bend its long, slender legs until it can get its mouth to the water. This looks very awkward and uncomfortable.

Giraffes have good sight, hearing and smell, and can also run very fast. Their blotchy brown markings help them to blend in with the background. If a giraffe is attacked it kicks out with its sharp hooves.

Because giraffes are so tall, they make good sentries or guards. Other animals, such as zebras, travel with the giraffe herd for protection.

Africa

The pelican

Pelicans are among the largest of the birds and are found in many parts of the world. Pelican fossils which date back forty million years have been found.

The pelican's main food is fish. It uses its large, pouched bill to scoop up the water and trap the fish. A pelican's beak can hold as much as thirty pints of water. Pelicans usually fish in groups. Sometimes they splash and paddle in the water, driving shoals of fish into shallow areas where they can be caught.

Pelicans nest in colonies which are often several miles away from the feeding area. One colony can contain as many as 40,000 birds.

The mother pelican swallows the fish and then brings it back into her beak for her young to eat. This makes it easier for the babies to digest.

Africa

The chimpanzee

The chimpanzee lives in the equatorial rain forests in the heart of Africa. It spends much of its time in the trees, but comes down to find food. Sometimes the chimpanzee steals grapefruit and melons from local farms.

A chimpanzee's hands are very like human hands. The thumb can move in all directions, which is rare in the animal world. The chimp can use its hands to perform all kinds of tasks. It can peel fruit properly, and use a stick to stir up an ant's nest.

Chimpanzees live in groups. They like to play, and they spend a lot of time grooming each other.

The young chimpanzee stays with its mother for two years. Male chimps then form their own groups, but females stay with their mothers.

Africa

The zebra

The zebra looks very similar to a horse, but no one has ever been able to tame a zebra. It is a very nervous, shy animal, always on the alert for danger from lions or leopards.

Zebras graze in large herds on the plains of Africa. They drink at waterholes in the evenings and they are especially careful during this time, ready to run at the least noise.

The zebra's black and white stripes make the animal stand out during the day. At night, however, a herd of zebras looks like grayish mounds of earth.

The zebras in this picture are Grant's zebras. They are the smallest species of zebra.

Africa

The leopard

The leopard is one of the big cats that live in the forests of Africa. It prefers to live in trees, and will often kill its prey by jumping on it from an overhanging branch. Leopards prefer to hunt at night. They will kill almost anything, from a lizard to an ox.

The leopard's golden tan coat is covered with black spots, and no two leopards have identical coats.

The male leopard weighs about 300 pounds, and the female up to 150 pounds. They are the third largest member of the cat family.

The leopard cub is ready to fend for itself when it is about a year old.

Africa

The mongoose

There are several different species of mongoose. The smallest is the dwarf mongoose. This tiny animal hunts in a pack with other mongooses, and feeds on insects, birds' eggs and small snakes. They call to each other with little bird-like sounds.

The white-tailed mongoose is the best known mongoose. It has a long, tufted white tail, large eyes and rounded ears. It hunts rats and snakes and, when they meet, the mongoose's eyes turn red and its fur stands on end.

Mongooses are very quick and are able to jump out of the way when a snake strikes with its poisonous fangs. For a long time, people believed that mongooses were not affected by a snake's poison, but that is not true. Their speed and agility just keeps them from being bitten.

The ancient Egyptians kept mongooses as pets and to rid the grain ships of rats.

135

Africa

The African elephant

The African elephant is the largest land mammal in the world and can weigh six tons. It has especially large ears, which is the main difference between the African and the Indian elephant. The African elephant is not easily tamed, so it is not used for work in the way that Indian elephants are.

The elephant's trunk is very sensitive and is used to pick things up, to pluck leaves from trees, and to carry water to its mouth. When an African elephant comes to a water hole, it can be heard drinking from far away as it squirts water down its throat.

An elephant's teeth are very strange. It has only one huge tooth in each jaw. As this is worn down, another grows forward to replace it.

An elephant's tusks are huge teeth, and can be used as weapons when danger threatens.

Africa

The gorilla

Many stories are told of the savage gorilla, that beats its chest before charging its enemy. However, the truth is that this huge ape is a calm, quiet animal that lives entirely on fruit and leaves. It lives in the African forests but is too heavy to spend much time in the trees, except at night when it sleeps. It walks on all fours, but stands upright if danger threatens.

Gorillas live in groups of about twenty. They have a leader, who makes sure that his followers obey the rules of the group. The tribe lives in its own part of the forest to make sure there is no trouble with neighboring groups.

The baby gorilla is carried in its mother's arms for the first two months of its life, and still enjoys a ride even when it is older.

Africa

The ostrich

The ostrich is the largest bird living today. It stands over six feet high and, with its long neck and legs, it is a very impressive sight.

Ostriches live in small flocks on the grasslands of Africa. Other animals like to graze near ostriches because they are very good at alerting them to danger. Ostriches eat all kinds of plants and fruit as well as lizards, small tortoises and rodents.

The ostrich feathers of black and white are very soft and have often been used to decorate clothes and hats. They have been hunted so much that in some areas, such as Arabia, there are no ostriches left at all.

All the hen ostriches of a flock lay their eggs in one nest, which is just a hollow in the ground.

Africa

The oryx

The oryx lives in the Kalahari Desert which is a very dry and barren place. Its hooves are specially shaped so that it can walk over the sand without sinking into it.

Oryxes can go for weeks without water if none can be found. This is because it never sweats when the sun is at its hottest, and so it does not lose any body moisture. To keep cool, the oryx pants as the temperature rises. If there is no water, the oryx drinks the dew to quench its thirst.

The oryx's long horns are very sharp and are used as weapons to protect itself and its young.

When the sun is at its highest, the oryx finds shelter under a rock or bush.

143

Africa

The hippopotamus

The hippopotamus is known as the 'river horse', because it spends the day in the water to keep cool and to avoid getting sunburn. It surfaces to breathe, with lots of snorting and ear-flicking. It is a large bulky animal, but can swim surprisingly fast, both on the surface and the bottom of the river.

The hippopotamus' nostrils are placed on top of its broad snout so that it can still breathe when the rest of its body is under the water.

A baby hippopotamus is born under the water. Ten minutes after its birth, the baby is able to swim alongside its mother.

Hippopotamuses leave the water at night to eat grass by the river bank.

145

Africa

The scaly anteater

The scaly anteater has a very unusual tube-shaped mouth. Inside the mouth, a long, sticky tongue lies curled up in its own special case. The anteater digs into a termite hill and the insects run out. Then the anteater shoots out its tongue and mops them up. An anteater has no teeth at all.

The scaly anteater uses its long tail as an extra hand. When it climbs trees, it wraps its tail around the branches to help it balance.

The scaly anteater can grow to be six feet long. It will not fight but runs away from its enemies.

While it is eating, the scaly anteater also picks up grains of sand, which it uses to digest its food.

Africa

The lion

The lion is called the 'king of the jungle', but this is not a true title because it lives on the plains and not in the jungles of Africa.

Lions live in groups called prides. Female lions or lionesses do most of the hunting and work together to track their prey. They spend a long time stalking the animal before rushing in for the kill. Even though the lionesses do the hunting, the male lion always eats first.

The male has a magnificent mane which takes about six years to fully grow. An adult male can weigh 500 pounds. However, it is a rather lazy animal and spends most of its time sleeping.

Lion cubs weigh about three pounds when they are born. Unlike domestic kittens, lion cubs can see from birth.

Africa

The Cape buffalo

The Cape buffalo is a very dangerous animal because it will attack without warning. It will even hide in bushes and then charge out at its enemy. The buffalo's broad horns are useful weapons.

The Cape buffalo has a special friend. This is a small, white heron called the cattle egret. It hops along the buffalo's back, picking off the flies and insects.

Cape buffaloes have another way of getting rid of troublesome pests. They wallow in mud until they are covered with slime. Then they rub against trees to scrape off the caked mud and the insects with it.

The calves are born at the end of the dry season when there is lots of grass to eat.

Africa

The okapi

The okapi is related to the giraffe, and lives in the deepest parts of the Congo forest. Its dark brown fur and striped legs help it to blend in with the undergrowth.

The okapi is so shy and timid that it was not discovered by white explorers until early in the twentieth century. Scientists have now found that the okapi is very similar to an extinct animal that lived millions of years ago. The resemblance is so close that the okapi is called a 'living fossil'.

Male okapis live alone in the jungle until they find mates. Okapis live only in certain parts of the rain forests. They always travel along the same paths, which the African Pygmies call 'okapi trails'.

An okapi foal has a short, stubby mane, but this falls out, so the adult okapi does not have one.

Oceania

The koala bear

The koala bear is a marsupial. This means that its baby is born when it is still not properly formed. The baby then climbs into its mother's pouch and stays there until it is big enough to start feeding itself. A baby koala stays in its mother's pouch for six months.

Koala bears are only found in the eucalyptus trees of Australia. Eucalyptus is used to make cold cures and the smell and taste are very strong. Because the koala only eats eucalyptus, they taste very nasty so other animals do not hunt them. The koalas' worst enemy is man, who hunts them for their fur.

The koala is a calm, quiet animal. It moves very slowly through the trees, clinging with its strong claws.

Oceania

The frilled lizard

The frilled lizard looks just like a dinosaur of long ago. It runs on its hind legs, and flicks its tail from side to side to balance itself. Adult frilled lizards can grow up to three feet long. They look quite frightening although they are harmless.

When a frilled lizard is angry or alarmed, it will pump blood into the frill that lies along its neck. This makes the frill stiffen, so the lizard's head looks much bigger than it is. The lizard will bare its teeth and hiss threateningly. However, if this does not frighten the enemy away, the lizard will turn tail and run for cover.

Lizards only eat insects, so they live mostly in trees where they can find plenty of food.

Baby lizards hatch from eggs. As soon as they are born, they can run and catch their own food.

Oceania

The dingo

The dingo is the wild dog of Australia. It looks just like an ordinary dog, but it is not able to bark.

Dingoes sleep in their dens during the day and go out to hunt at night. They catch their prey by chasing it until the animal is worn out and can no longer run. Dingoes often hunt sheep, so farmers do not hesitate to shoot them.

Dingoes live in packs, and they all share the food that is caught.

Oceania

The emu

The emu is the second largest bird on earth. It can grow up to six feet in height. Although it cannot fly, the emu runs very fast, reaching speeds of up to thirty five miles an hour. As well as being able to run away from danger, the emu also uses its powerful legs to kick out at its enemies.

After the female emu lays her eggs, she takes no more interest in them. The male emu then takes over, and sits on the eggs for two months until they hatch.

The male emu also cares for the chicks once they have hatched. He looks after them while they feed, and at night he gathers the chicks under his wings to keep them warm.

Emus enjoy different kinds of food, such as insects, berries, seeds and grubs.

160

Oceania

The tiger shark

A tiger shark belongs to a very ancient species of fish. Sharks have been in existence for 250 million years. Sharks are unusual because their skeletons are not made of bone but of muscle and gristle. They do not have scales, but their skin is covered with sharp points, which are exactly like teeth.

The tiger shark is one of the smaller sharks, growing to about twelve feet long. However, it is a very fierce hunter, and because it hunts in packs, it is sometimes called the wolf of the sea.

When a baby tiger shark is born, it is pale brown with dark stripes. As it grows, its color changes to a grayish-brown.

Oceania

The kangaroo

The kangaroo is a marsupial and, like the koala bear, its baby is born before it is fully formed. A baby kangaroo is only about an inch long, it is bald and blind, and its back legs do not work. Yet somehow it manages to climb into its mother's pouch where it finds food and warmth.

Kangaroos are grazing animals and roam the grasslands of Australia. They have very strong back legs and can bound up to forty miles an hour in great leaps. They use their long, thick tails as weights to balance themselves.

Kangaroos live in herds, and the most experienced kangaroo is the leader.

Oceania

The duck-billed platypus

The duck-billed platypus is a very peculiar creature. It is a mammal, but lays eggs like a reptile. It has short, thick hair; broad, webbed feet; and a soft, feathery bill. The female platypus feeds her babies, but they do not suck. Instead, they lap up the milk which oozes from special glands inside the mother.

The female platypus digs out a long tunnel in a river bank and makes a nest at the end, using wet leaves. She lays two eggs and stays with them for about ten days until they hatch. The babies then climb into their mother's pouch. They stay in the pouch for two months, and it is a long time after that before they are ready to look after themselves.

Duck-billed platypuses are slow and clumsy on land, but they are fast swimmers and good divers. The platypus has a small flap over its eyes that protects them underwater.

Platypuses eat an amazing amount
of worms and shellfish. In the
Bronx Zoo in New York, three
people were employed just to
provide food for the platypuses.

Oceania

The black swan

The black swan is found only in the wild in Australia and Tasmania, although it has been introduced to ornamental ponds in Europe and America. It is very striking with its black feathers, bright red beak and white wing tips.

The black swan builds its nest from twigs and dead leaves. The nest is hidden in the reeds at the water's edge. The female, or pen, sits on her eggs for about a month.

Baby swans are called cygnets. They learn to fly when they are about six months old and then they find their own section of the river to live in.

If the cygnets get tired when they are swimming, the mother swan carries them on her back.

Sugar gliders stay in their mother's pouch for about two months until their fur grows.

Oceania

The sugar glider

The sugar glider is another of the Australian marsupials. It builds its nest at the top of eucalyptus trees. The nest is made with roughly woven twigs and branches lined with dead leaves, and is about the size of a soccer ball.

Sugar gliders have large folds of skin that join their front and back legs. When they jump from a high branch, they spread their arms and legs and the skin acts as a kind of parachute. The sugar glider can travel up to 150 feet at a time which allows it to cover the forest quickly in its search for fruits and nuts. Its favorite food is the sweet sap from the manna gum tree.

Oceania

The elephant seal

Elephant seals are huge animals. The adult male grows to a length of more than twenty feet, and weighs several tons. When it is angry, the seal's nose swells up, and so it is given its other name of sea elephant.

In spite of its size, the elephant seal is a very peaceful animal.

Baby elephant seals weigh almost a hundred pounds but they need their mothers to look after them. The mother elephant seal will go without food for days at a time so that she does not have to leave her pup for too long.

The elephant seal is a clumsy creature on land, but it is a good swimmer.

Oceania

The cockatoo

The cockatoo lives in large flocks. If one cockatoo is in trouble, it gives a distress call and other members of the flock come to its aid. When the flock searches for seeds, nuts and berries, one or two cockatoos remain on guard duty in the surrounding trees.

Cockatoos live for a long time. One bird kept in a zoo lived for about 100 years. Cockatoos are also very clever at mimicking noises made by other animals.

Baby cockatoos are not very beautiful when they first hatch, but the adult bird has lovely white feathers and a yellow crest.

Cockatoos build their nests in holes in tree trunks. They use their sharp beaks to make the holes larger.

Oceania

The wombat

The wombat is another member of the marsupial family. It is nearsighted, has very strong, curved claws, and sharp teeth. The wombat's squat body and short, thick legs are ideal for burrowing the tunnels in which it lives.

The female wombat uses her claws to dig a tunnel. She hides in it during the day and leaves her baby safely there alone after it is able to live outside her pouch.

The tunnel is not deep but can be as long as seventy feet. The wombat makes sure that there are several different exits so that it can escape in times of danger. When tree roots block the tunnel, a wombat quickly gnaws through them. A wombat's teeth grow all the time, so they do not get worn away by all the chewing.

Wombats are vegetarians. They eat grass, roots and the inner bark of trees.

Oceania

The tree kangaroo

The tree kangaroo makes its home in the wooded hillsides of Queensland, Australia. It probably developed from a ground-living animal that started to climb trees for safety. Now its legs have adapted to life in the trees, and its feet have rough pads on the soles to help them grip the trees. Its tail has also changed, and is used to balance the tree kangaroo as it sits in the branches eating leaves.

Tree kangaroos spend most of the day sleeping in the trees. At dusk they move backwards down the trees to find a stream to drink from.

The tree kangaroos will stay in one place until they have eaten all the fruit and leaves and then they move on.

A baby tree kangaroo stays in its mother's pouch for several months. As soon as it leaves, another new-born baby takes its place.

Oceania

The kiwi

The kiwi is a flightless bird that lives in New Zealand. Kiwis are nocturnal – they hunt for their food at night. Kiwis' bills have the nostrils at the tips, giving them a very good sense of smell. They can find insects, grubs and worms by sniffing them out. Then they use their long bills to dig out their supper.

Kiwis nest in burrows. The female, who is larger than the male, lays one, chalky-white egg about six inches across. The male then takes over and sits on it for about eighty days until the chick hatches.

The kiwi chick is taught how to hunt for worms by its father.

Oceania

The spotted cuscus

Despite its name, the only spots on a spotted cuscus are found on the male. The females and babies have no markings on their grayish-yellow coats. They are nocturnal animals, spending the days hanging from the branches by their tails. At night they go hunting for lizards and snails.

Fully grown spotted cuscuses are rather sluggish, slow animals. The young cuscuses are much more lively and often run up and down the trees, chasing small animals. The adults are hardy, brave creatures. If one is wounded, it hides away until it is healed.

Cuscuses do not like being touched and give off a foul-smelling scent when they are stroked.

The king penguin stands about three feet high and is a very powerful swimmer.

Oceania

The king penguin

There are seventeen or eighteen species of penguins. The king penguin is one of the largest penguins. It does not make a nest in which to lay its eggs. The penguin rests the egg on top of its feet abd covers it with the warm skin of its belly.

The female and male both take their turn in keeping the egg warm. The males do most of the work, however. During the sixty days it takes before the egg hatches, the males lose about a third of their body weight, because they cannot search for food. If the eggs are left for a minute, the chicks inside will die.

Oceania

The Tasmanian devil

The Tasmanian devil lives only in Tasmania, an island off the south coast of Australia. This meat-eating marsupial catches rats, mice, crabs, frogs and other small animals. It looks like a cross between a bear and a badger and is the size of a large domestic cat. The Tasmanian devil has sharp, pointed teeth, and a reputation for being very bad-tempered. These animals are in danger of becoming extinct. They are hunted by farmers, and their feeding grounds have gradually been used up for farmland.

The female Tasmanian devil builds a nest for the young when they are old enough to leave the pouch.

186

Oceania

The albatross

The albatross is a large bird that travels over the southern oceans of the world. Its long, slender wings catch the draughts of air rising from the waves, allowing it to keep aloft with little or no movement of its wings. The albatross can travel great distances. One bird is known to have traveled thousands of miles from its own area.

Albatrosses live in colonies. They return to the same site year after year, and each one repairs the nest it used the year before. The female lays one egg a year. When the chicks are old enough to look after themselves, the colony splits up. Each albatross goes its own way until the next year.

188

Albatrosses live mainly on cuttlefish and squid that rise to the surface of the ocean at night.

Oceania

The numbat

The numbat is also known as the banded anteater, although it prefers to eat termites. It has a very keen sense of smell, and can easily find the huge termite mounds that dot the Australian countryside. It rips open the side of the mound with its sharp claws and licks up the termites with its long, sticky tongue. An adult numbat can eat between 10,000 and 20,000 termites a day.

The numbat is a marsupial, but in this case, the mother's pouch is very shallow. The babies have to cling to the long hairs on her stomach in order to get their milk. The young leave their mother after only a month and quickly learn how to find their own food.

The numbat feeds by day, keeping a watchful eye open for its main enemy, the dingo.